AF270500

RONDA ROUSEY

A&D Xtreme
BOLD HI-LO NONFICTION
An imprint of Abdo Publishing
abdobooks.com

ALEX MONNIG

TAKE IT TO THE XTREME!

GET READY FOR AN EXTREME ADVENTURE! THE PAGES OF THIS BOOK WILL TAKE YOU INTO THE THRILLING WORLD OF PROFESSIONAL WRESTLING. WHEN YOU HAVE FINISHED READING THIS BOOK, TAKE THE XTREME CHALLENGE ON PAGE 45 ABOUT WHAT YOU'VE LEARNED!

ABDOBOOKS.COM

Published by Abdo Publishing, a division of ABDO, PO Box 398166, Minneapolis, Minnesota 55439. Copyright © 2024 by Abdo Consulting Group, Inc. International copyrights reserved in all countries. No part of this book may be reproduced in any form without written permission from the publisher. A&D Xtreme™ is a trademark and logo of Abdo Publishing.

Printed in the United States of America, North Mankato, MN.

052023
092023

Design: Kelly Doudna, Mighty Media, Inc.

Production: Mighty Media, Inc.

Editor: Katherine Chu

Cover Photograph: MediaPunch Master/AP Images

Interior Photographs: A.RICARDO/Shutterstock Images, pp. 12–13; Charles Dharapak/AP Images, pp. 10–11; David Becker/AP Images, pp. 14–15; George Napolitano/AP Images, pp. 1, 16–17, 28–29, 30–31, 32–33, 42–43, 44; Independent Photo Agency Srl/Alamy Photo, pp. 22–23, 34–35; IPA/Alamy Photo, p. 39; Jeff Kravitz/Getty Images, pp. 36–37; MediaPunch Inc/Alamy Photo, pp. 40–41; Miguel Discart/Flickr, pp. 4–5, 20–21; Miguel Discart/Wikimedia Commons, pp. 26–27; REUTERS/Alamy Photo, pp. 6–7; Silvia Izquierdo/AP Images, pp. 8–9; Star Shooter/AP Images, pp. 24–25; Wikimedia Commons, p. 38; Zuma Press, Inc./Alamy Photo, pp. 18–19

Design Elements: amgun/Shutterstock Images (perspective); sanchesnet1/iStockphoto (spikes color, bolts); Wth/Shutterstock Images (stripes)

LIBRARY OF CONGRESS CONTROL NUMBER: 2022948815

PUBLISHER'S CATALOGING-IN-PUBLICATION DATA

Names: Monnig, Alex, author.

Title: Ronda Rousey / by Alex Monnig

Description: Minneapolis, Minnesota : Abdo Publishing, 2024 | Series: Xtreme wrestling royalty | Includes online resources and index.

Identifiers: ISBN 9781098291495 (lib. bdg.) | ISBN 9781098277956 (ebook)

Subjects: LCSH: Rousey, Ronda--Juvenile literature. | Wrestlers--Biography--Juvenile literature. | Women wrestlers--Biography--Juvenile literature. | Women martial artists--Biography--Juvenile literature. | Actresses--Biography--Juvenile literature. | World Wrestling Entertainment, Inc--Juvenile literature.

Classification: DDC 796.812092--dc23

TABLE OF CONTENTS

CHAPTER 1

A STRONG START

Mixed **martial arts** (MMA) master Ronda Rousey was ready to fight. Dwayne "the Rock" Johnson brought her into the ring at WrestleMania XXXI in 2015. They faced Paul "Triple H" Levesque and Stephanie McMahon. All four wrestlers performed thrilling **stunts**. Rousey threw Triple H out of the ring then tossed McMahon to the mat. The crowd cheered as the Rock and Rousey bumped fists in celebration of their win.

The crowd chanted Ronda Rousey's (*top right*) name as the Rock (*left center*) brought her to face Stephanie McMahon (*bottom right*) and Triple H (*bottom left*).

CHAPTER 2

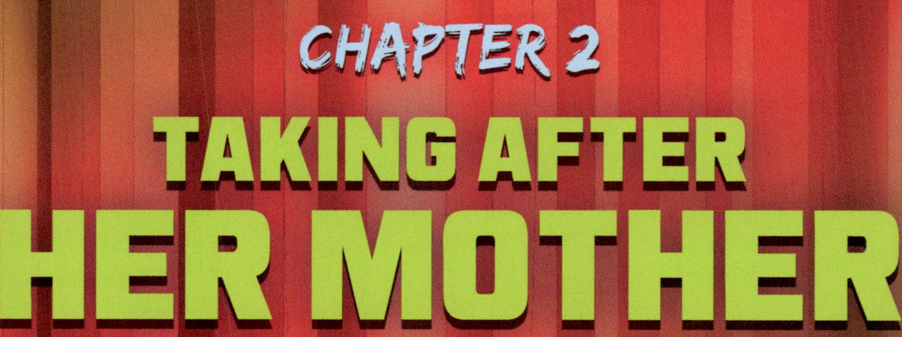

TAKING AFTER HER MOTHER

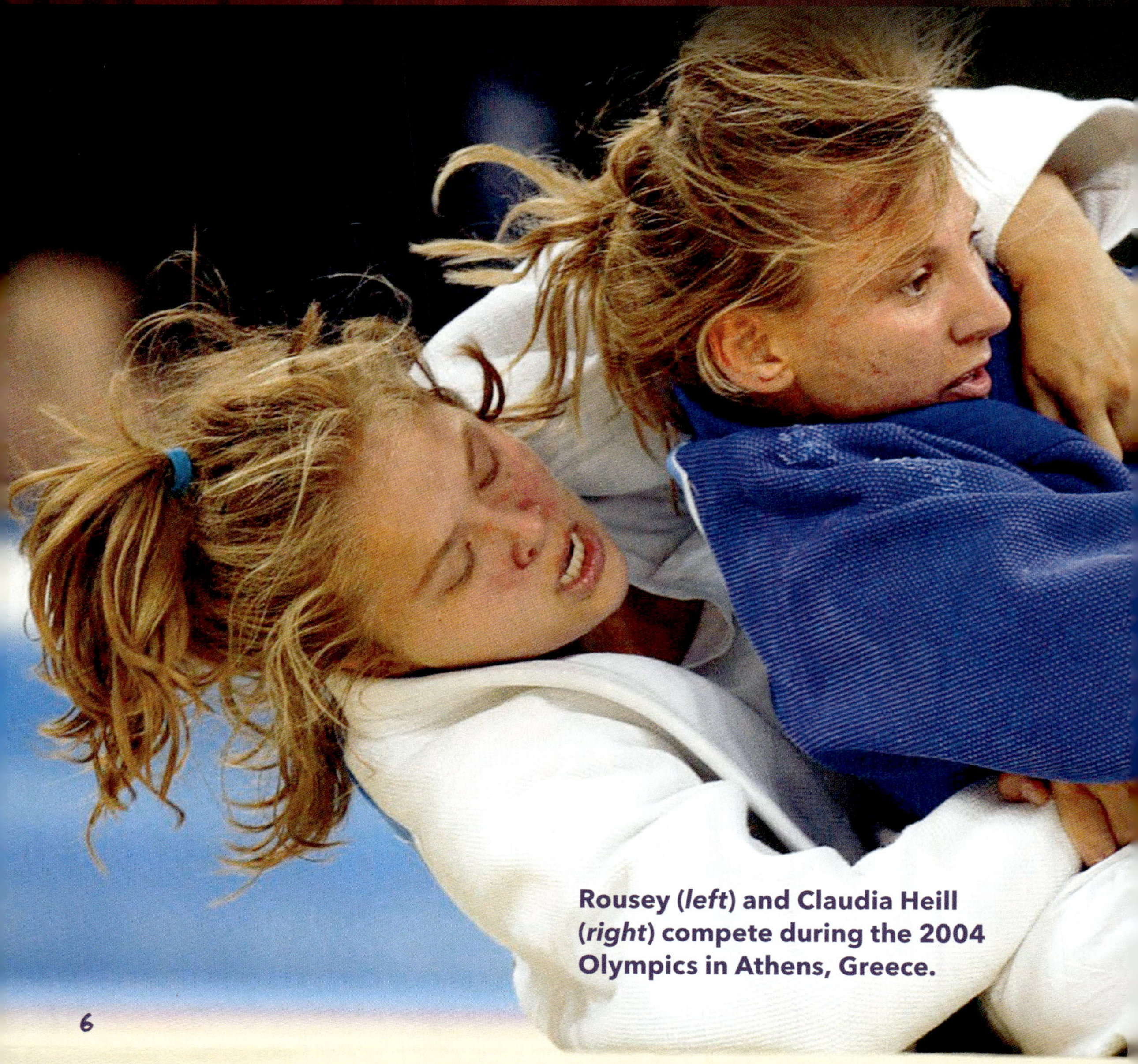

Rousey (*left*) and Claudia Heill (*right*) compete during the 2004 Olympics in Athens, Greece.

Ronda Jean Rousey was born on February 1, 1987, in Riverside, California. Her mother, AnnMaria DeMars, was a judoka. That means she competed in a combat sport called **judo**, a form of **martial arts**. DeMars became the first American judo world champion in 1984. In the 1990s, DeMars encouraged Ronda to try the sport.

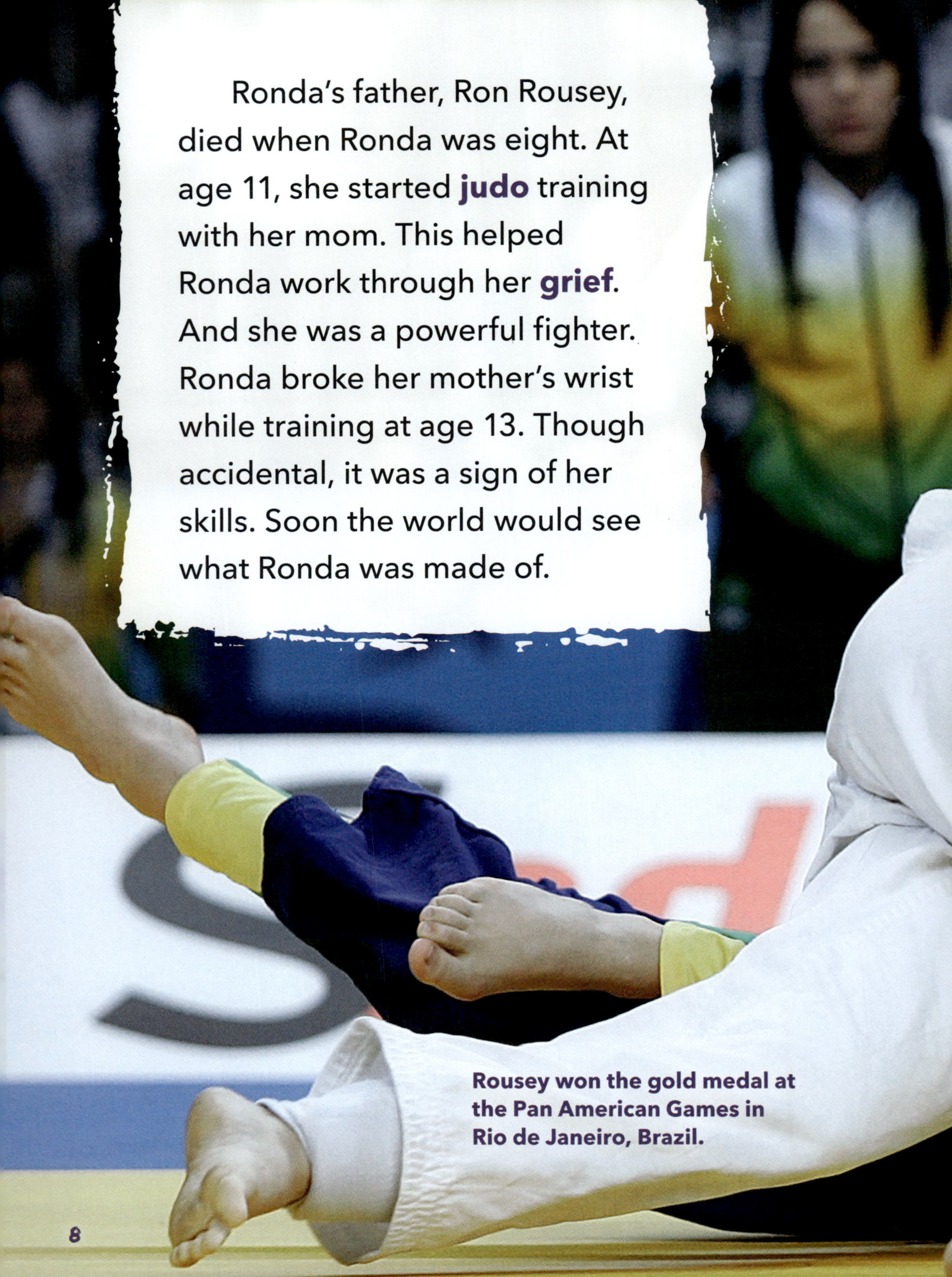

Ronda's father, Ron Rousey, died when Ronda was eight. At age 11, she started **judo** training with her mom. This helped Ronda work through her **grief**. And she was a powerful fighter. Ronda broke her mother's wrist while training at age 13. Though accidental, it was a sign of her skills. Soon the world would see what Ronda was made of.

Rousey won the gold medal at the Pan American Games in Rio de Janeiro, Brazil.

XTREME FACT

Ronda Rousey was born with apraxia, a condition that made speaking difficult. In 1990, Ronda's family moved to North Dakota so she could get speech therapy at Minot State University.

CHAPTER 3
BECOMING
A FIGHTER

At age 17, Ronda was the youngest of all the judoka competing in the 2004 **Olympics**. She didn't win any medals. But she returned to the 2008 Olympics ready to fight. Rousey won a bronze medal, becoming the first American to win an Olympic medal in women's **judo**. After that win, she was ready to try a new sport.

Rousey competes with Nasiba Surkieva during the 2008 Olympics in Beijing, China. Rousey's mom was her coach at the time.

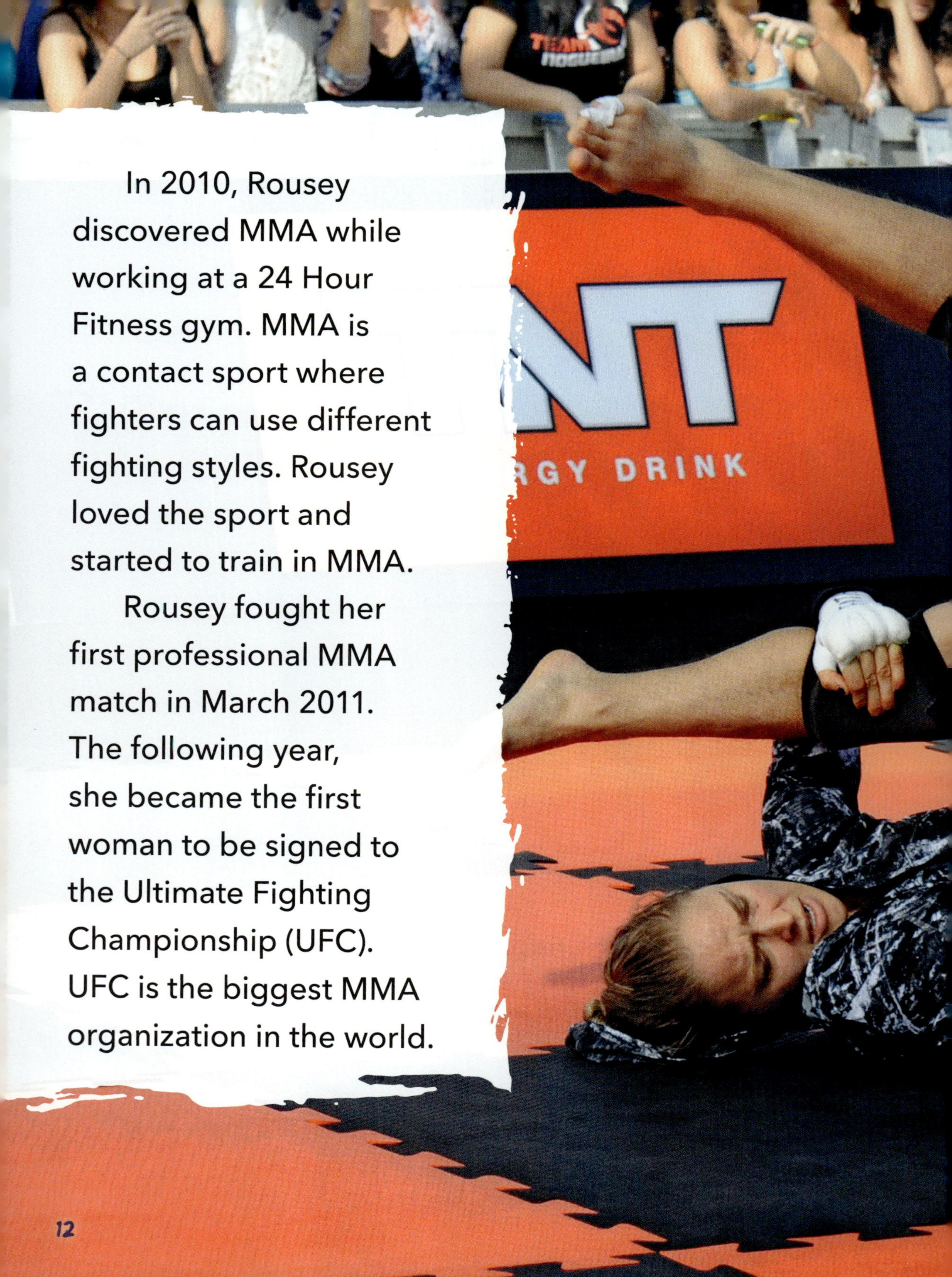

In 2010, Rousey discovered MMA while working at a 24 Hour Fitness gym. MMA is a contact sport where fighters can use different fighting styles. Rousey loved the sport and started to train in MMA.

Rousey fought her first professional MMA match in March 2011. The following year, she became the first woman to be signed to the Ultimate Fighting Championship (UFC). UFC is the biggest MMA organization in the world.

Rousey working out with a trainer before her UFC 190 match in Brazil in 2015

In 2013, Rousey (*right*) used her arm bar move on Miesha Tate (*left*) during UFC 168 in Las Vegas, Nevada. Rousey won six out of eight total UFC fights.

Rousey won 12 out of 14 MMA matches between 2011 and 2016. Many fans loved her arm bar submission hold. Rousey would grab her opponent's wrist and lay back, crossing her legs across their chest. She then pushed her hips against her opponent's elbow, painfully extending their arm. This made her opponent submit. Rousey often used this move to defeat opponents.

CHAPTER 4

A WRESTLING FAN

Rousey used the nickname "Rowdy" during her MMA career. The nickname originally belonged to World Wrestling Entertainment (WWE) wrestler Roderick "'Rowdy' Roddy Piper" Toombs. Rousey was a huge fan of Piper and WWE. WWE is a professional wrestling organization that features characters who perform in staged matches.

XTREME FACT

In 2018, Rousey became the first woman inducted into the UFC Hall of Fame.

Piper gave Rousey
permission to use
his nickname. Rousey
continued to use the
nickname after she
joined WWE.

In 2014, Rousey and three other MMA fighters attended WWE SummerSlam as fans. The group called themselves the Four Horsewomen. They sat in the front row and went **backstage** to meet the event's wrestlers, getting the media's attention. Reporters started to wonder if Rousey would leave MMA for WWE.

Rousey demonstrates a move at a clinic held by the Four Horsewomen. The Four Horsewomen taught fans different fighting techniques, led drills, took photos, and signed autographs.

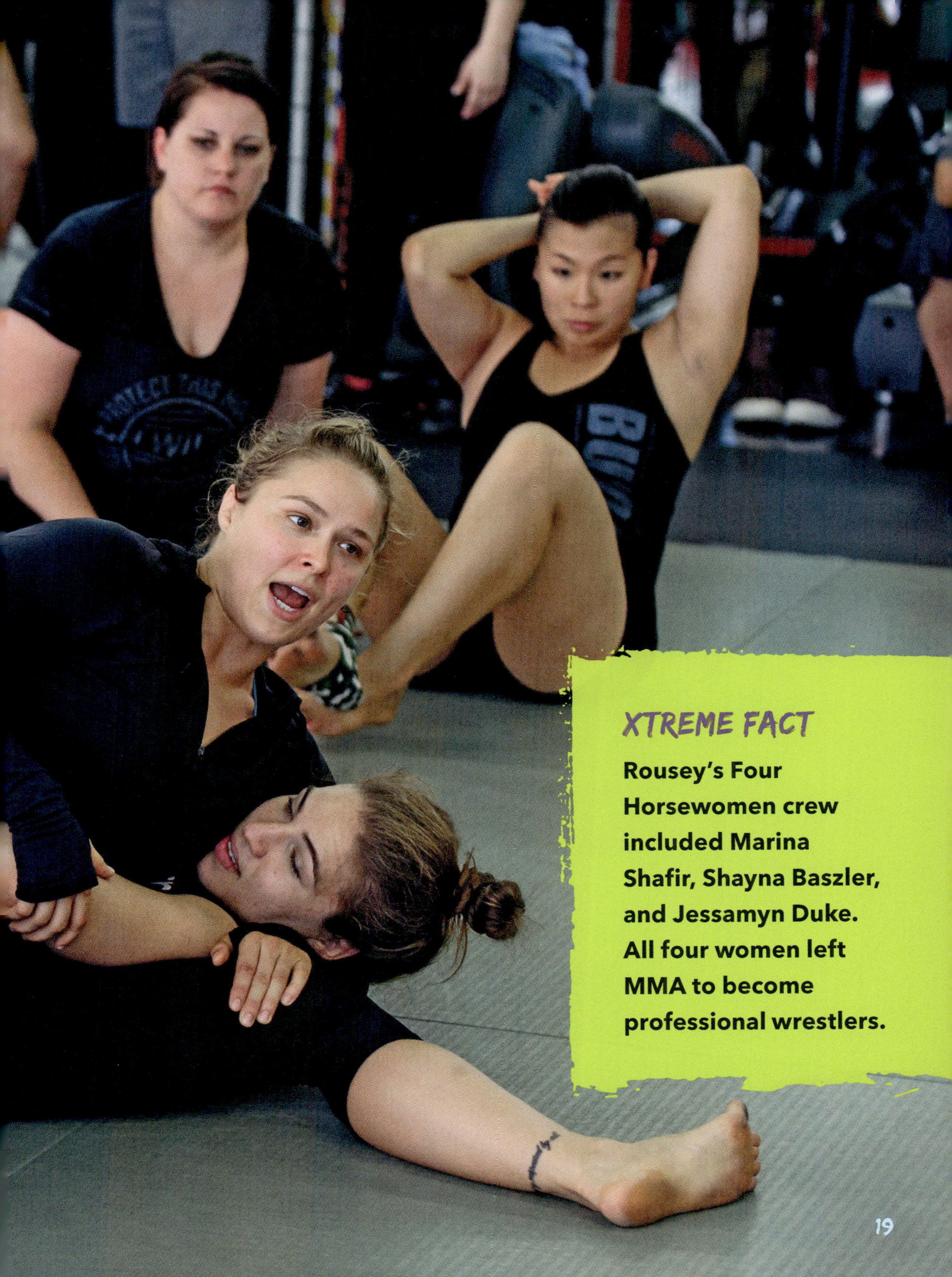

XTREME FACT

Rousey's Four
Horsewomen crew
included Marina
Shafir, Shayna Baszler,
and Jessamyn Duke.
All four women left
MMA to become
professional wrestlers.

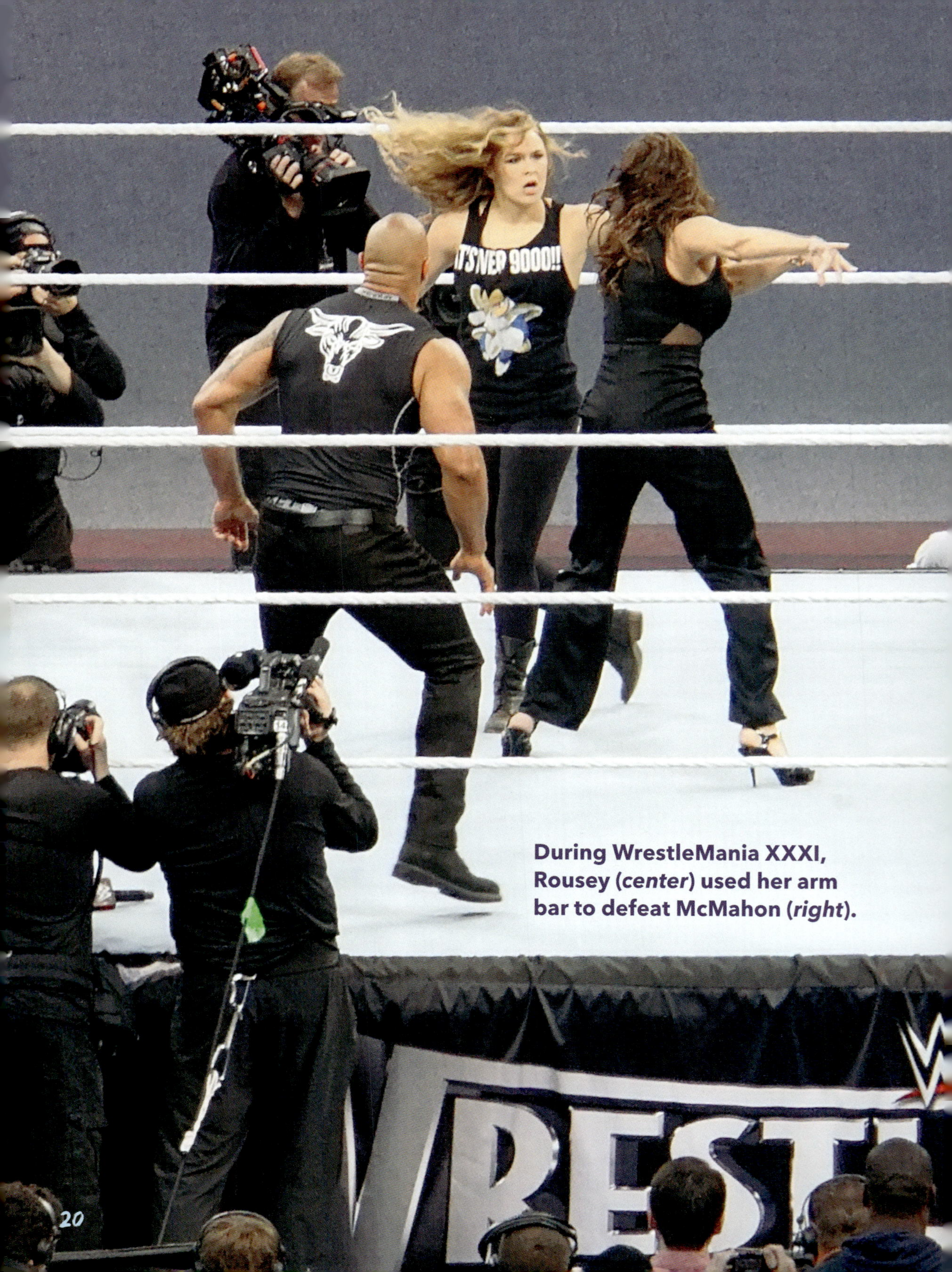

During WrestleMania XXXI, Rousey (*center*) used her arm bar to defeat McMahon (*right*).

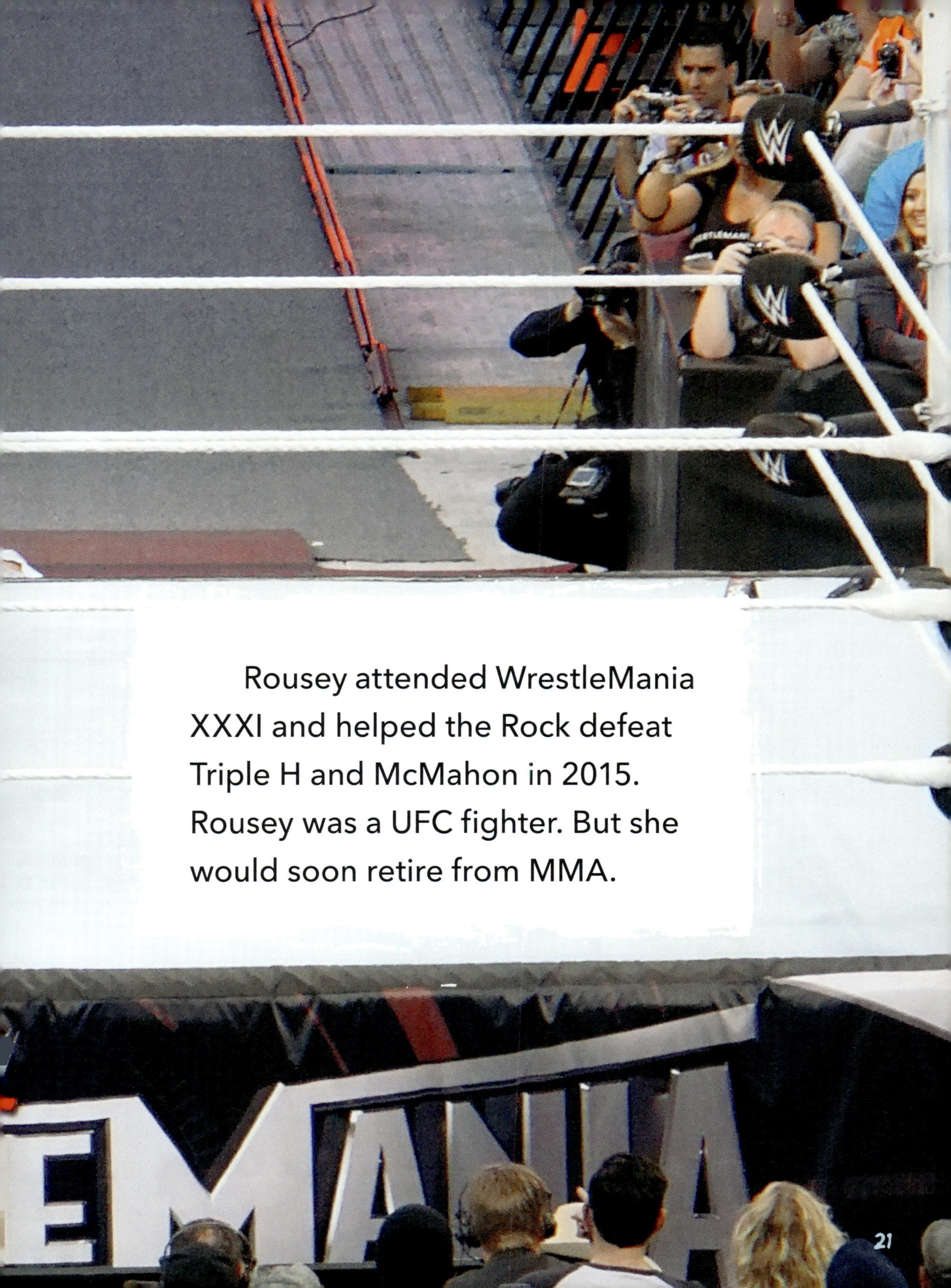

Rousey attended WrestleMania XXXI and helped the Rock defeat Triple H and McMahon in 2015. Rousey was a UFC fighter. But she would soon retire from MMA.

CROSSING OVER

Rousey made another surprise WWE appearance at the January 2018 Royal Rumble event. After the final match, Rousey entered the ring during the winners' victory celebration wearing Piper's black leather jacket in honor of his **legacy**.

Rousey's Piper's Pit move is inspired by
Piper. Rousey would carry her opponent
over her shoulders. Then she would fall
back, throwing them onto the mat.

Without saying a word, Rousey stared down the winners while pointing to a WrestleMania sign hanging in the **arena**. This meant she had officially joined WWE!

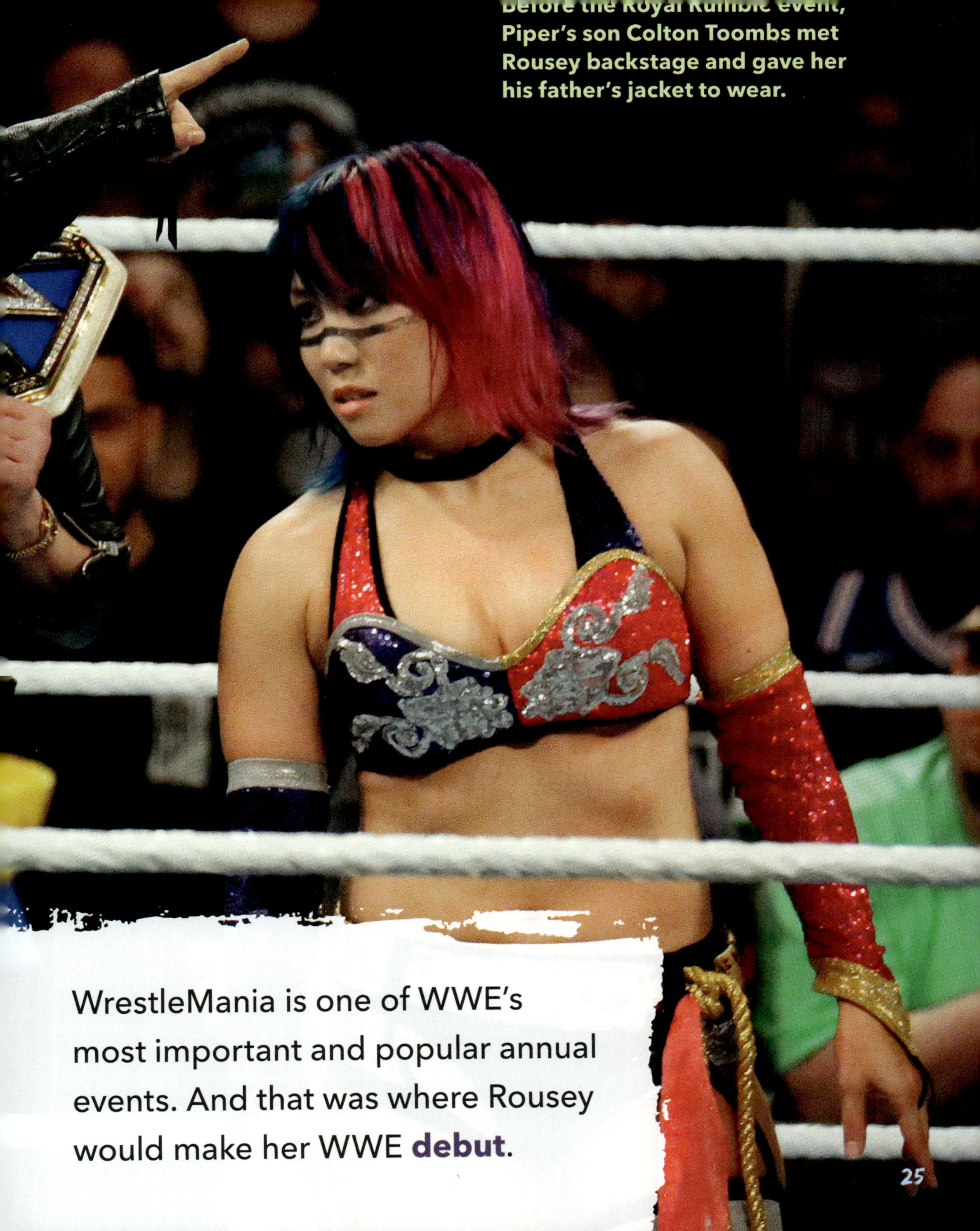

WrestleMania is one of WWE's most important and popular annual events. And that was where Rousey would make her WWE **debut**.

CHAPTER 6

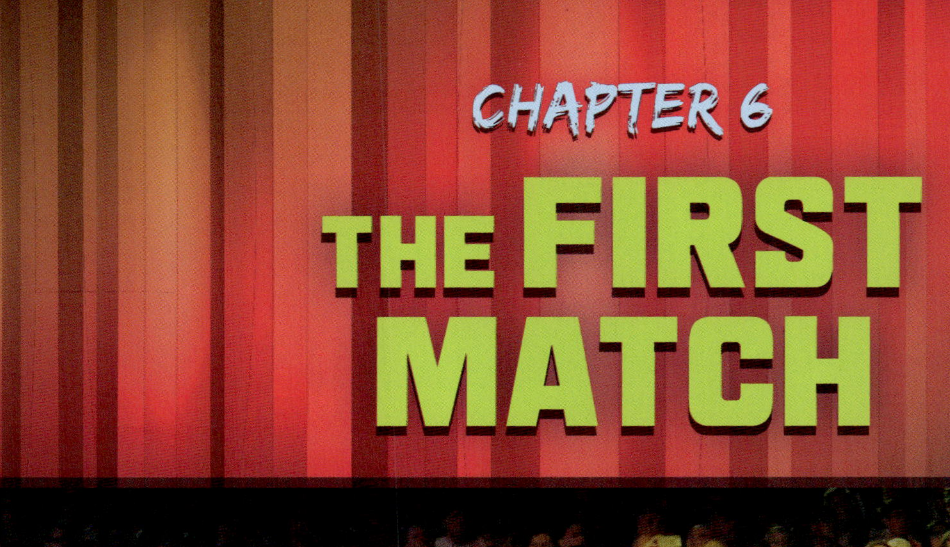

THE FIRST MATCH

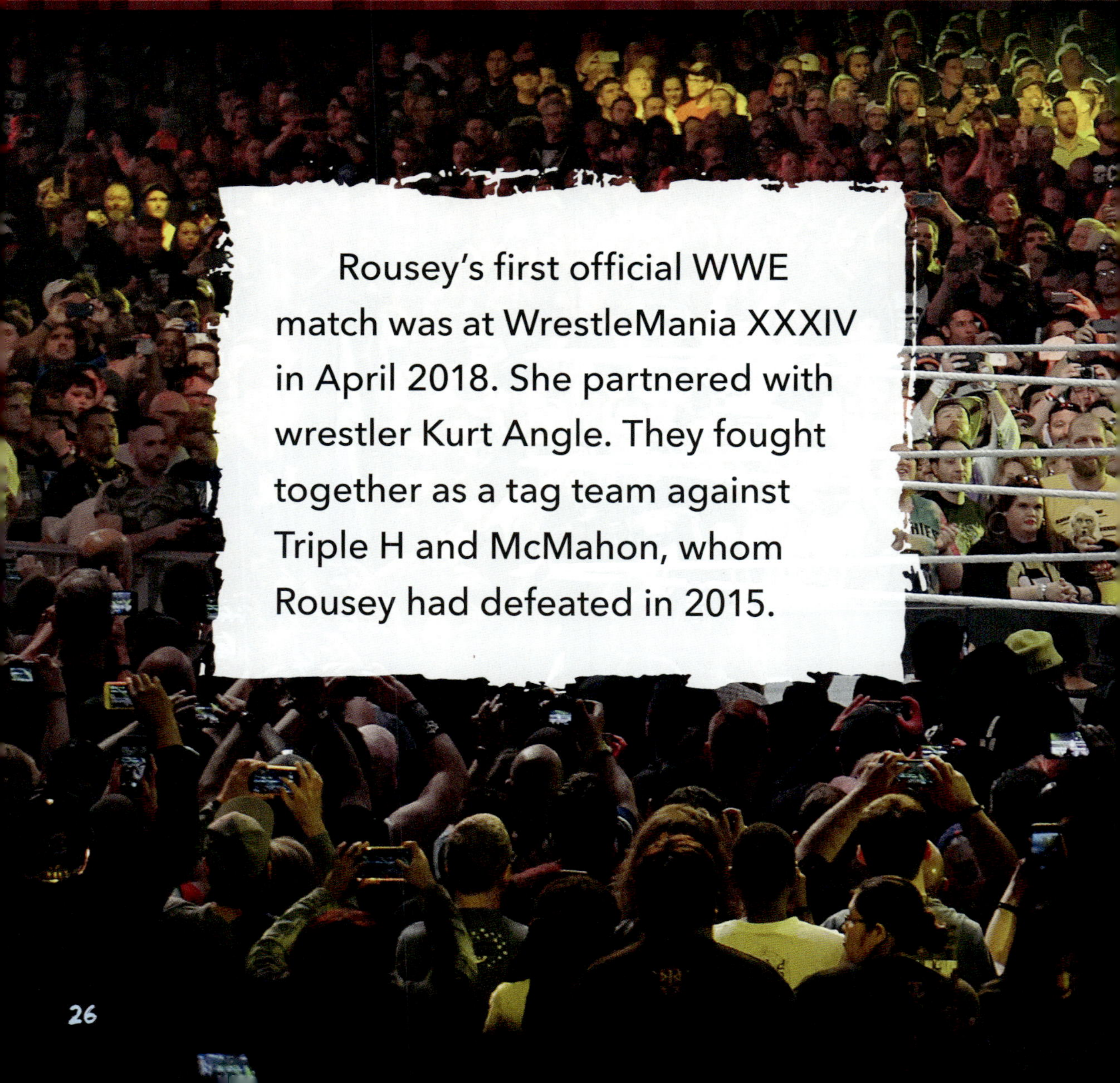

Rousey's first official WWE match was at WrestleMania XXXIV in April 2018. She partnered with wrestler Kurt Angle. They fought together as a tag team against Triple H and McMahon, whom Rousey had defeated in 2015.

Rousey with Kurt Angle (*center*) at WrestleMania XXXIV. Angle also mentored Rousey and helped guide her during her transition to WWE.

In a match full of strong wrestlers, Rousey stood out. She tossed McMahon around the ring as fans chanted, "This is awesome!" Rousey also **reversed** Triple H's finishing move before putting him in an arm bar. Then she forced McMahon to tap out. Rousey and Angle won! Rousey's WWE career was off to an exciting start.

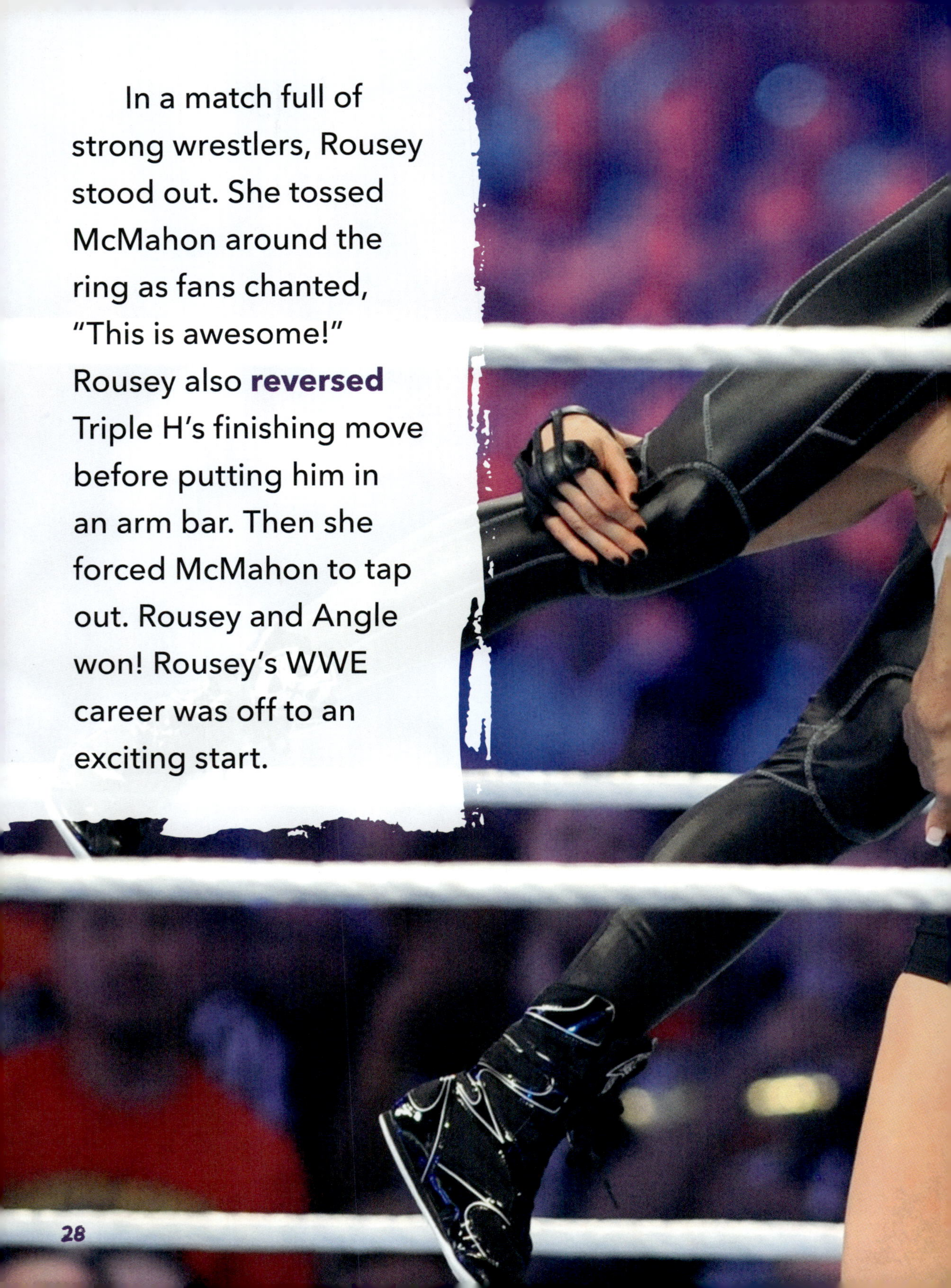

Rousey showed off her skills during WrestleMania XXXIV. She not only picked up McMahon but was also able to pick up Triple H too!

XTREME FACT

Rousey isn't the first athlete to compete in WWE and MMA. Ken Shamrock and Brock Lesnar have also competed in both sports.

CHAPTER 7

RISING QUICKLY

Rousey fought her first match without a partner in June 2018. She faced Savelina "Nia Jax" Fanene at the Money in the Bank event. But Alexis "Alexa Bliss" Cabrera interrupted the match. She defeated Rousey and Jax, winning the WWE Raw Women's Championship.

In 2018, Rousey easily beat Bliss using her arm bar move during SummerSlam.

Two months later, Rousey challenged Bliss for the championship title at SummerSlam. She defeated Bliss in four minutes to become the new WWE Raw Women's Champion!

Rousey celebrates her 2018 SummerSlam win with Stephanie "Nikki Bella" Garcia-Colace (*left*), Brianna "Brie Bella" Garcia-Colace (*second from right*), and Natalya Neidhart (*right*).

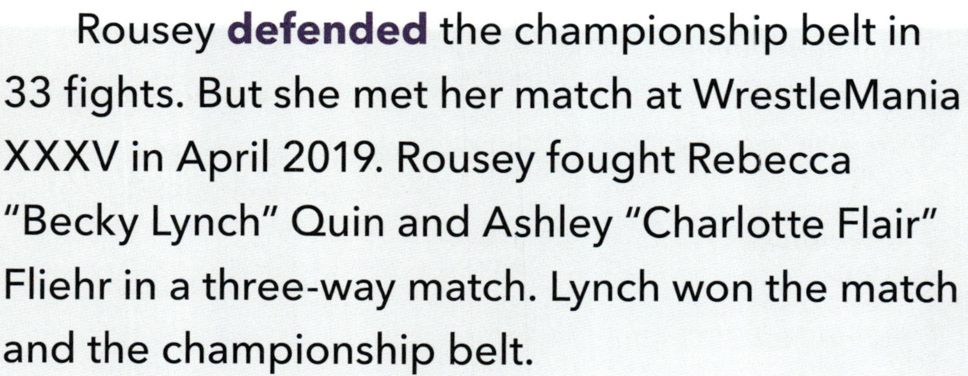

Rousey **defended** the championship belt in 33 fights. But she met her match at WrestleMania XXXV in April 2019. Rousey fought Rebecca "Becky Lynch" Quin and Ashley "Charlotte Flair" Fliehr in a three-way match. Lynch won the match and the championship belt.

Rousey held the WWE Raw Women's Championship title for 231 days in 2018. Her streak was beaten by Becky Lynch's record of 398 days, which started with Rousey's defeat at WrestleMania XXXV in 2019.

Rousey (*left*) defeated Mickie James (*right*) at WWE Live in Rome, Italy, in 2018.

CHAPTER 8

TAKING A BREAK

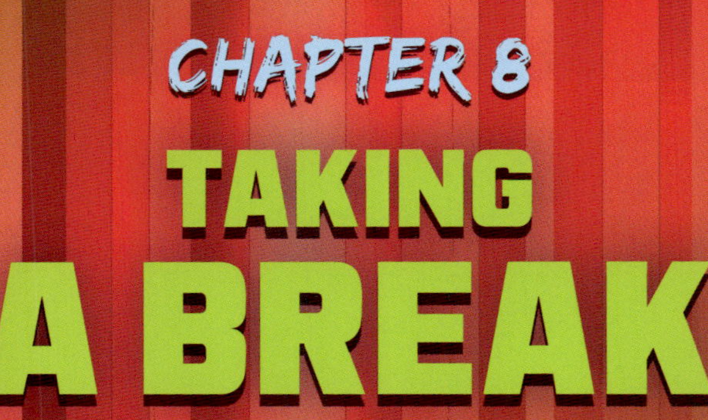

After losing to Lynch, Rousey took a break from wrestling. She was tired of traveling and competing 200 days a year. She also wanted to start a family. Rousey had married retired UFC fighter Travis Browne in 2017. In June 2021, they welcomed a daughter, La'akea Browne.

XTREME FACT

In 2017, Rousey and Travis Browne bought a farm called Browsey Acres. Rousey spends time there when she's not competing.

CHAPTER 9

COMING BACK STRONG

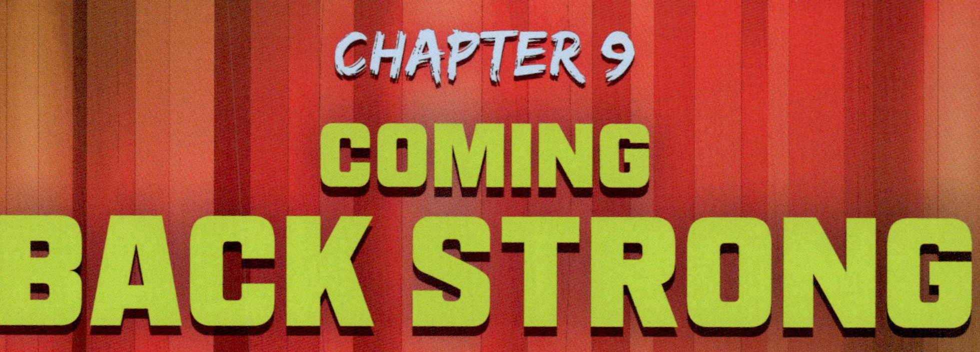

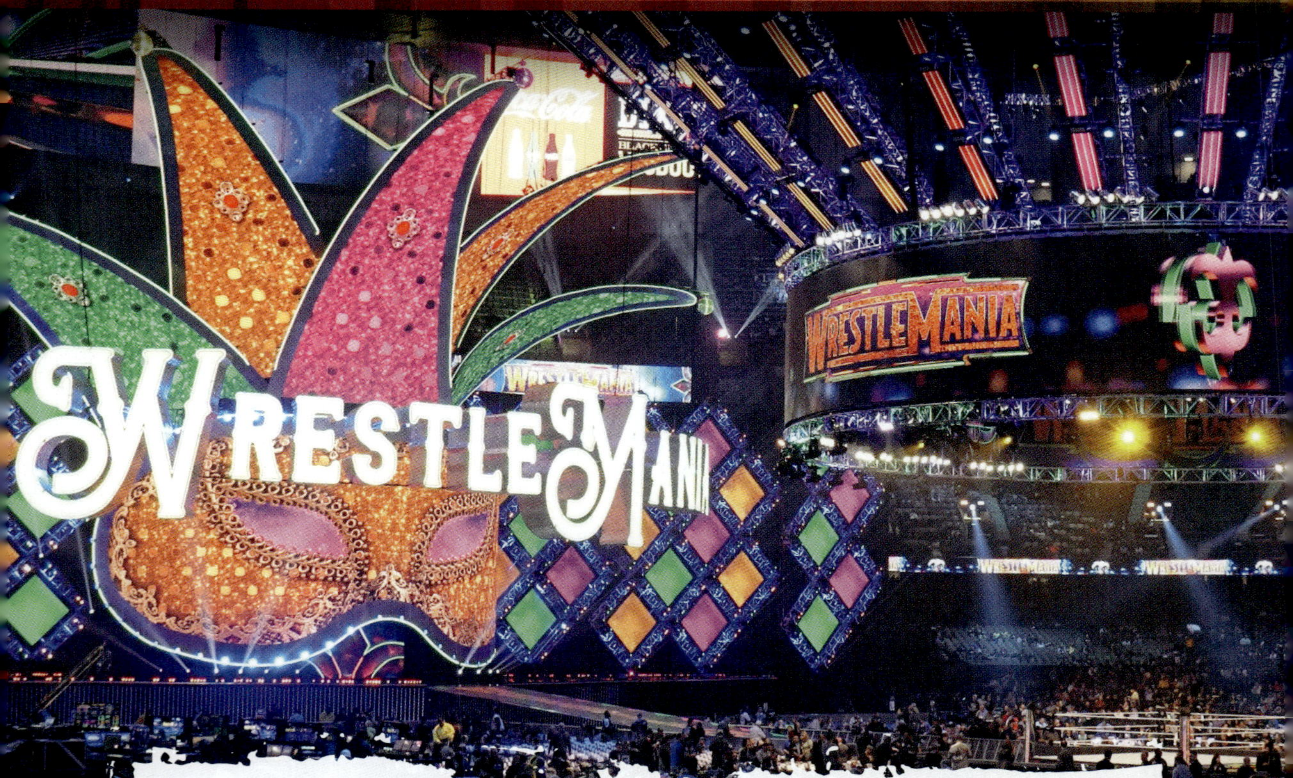

Rousey returned to WWE in January 2022, winning the Royal Rumble. That earned her a spot in the championship fight. Rousey lost to Flair at WrestleMania XXXVIII in April. But she didn't let that stop her from fighting back.

Since her first WrestleMania win in 2018, Rousey continued to win most of her WWE matches. She won 113 out of 128 fights between 2018 and 2022.

Bliss (*left*) did her best to avoid Rousey when they fought at SummerSlam in 2018. But once Rousey caught Bliss, Rousey easily defeated her.

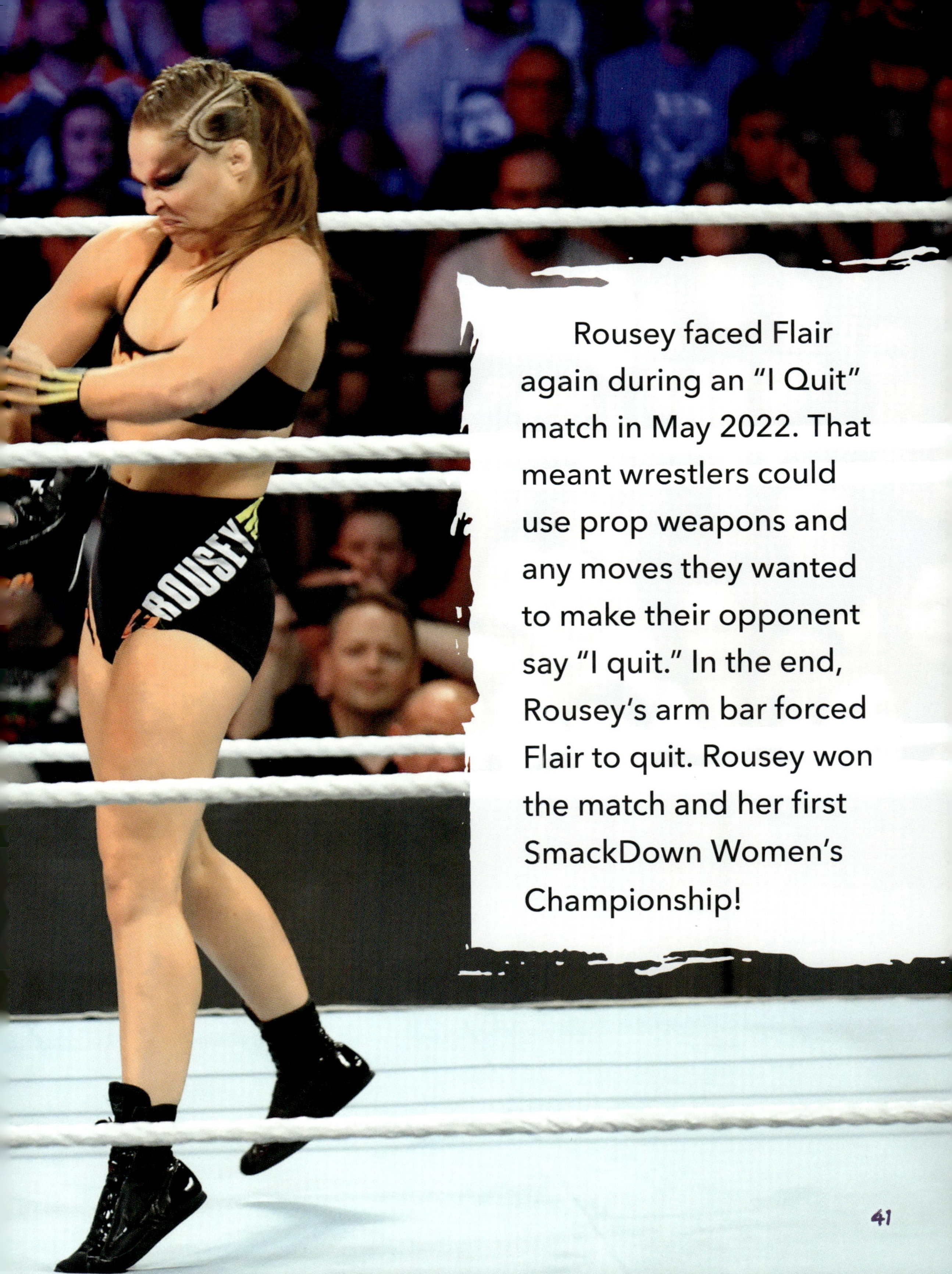

Rousey faced Flair again during an "I Quit" match in May 2022. That meant wrestlers could use prop weapons and any moves they wanted to make their opponent say "I quit." In the end, Rousey's arm bar forced Flair to quit. Rousey won the match and her first SmackDown Women's Championship!

Rousey's next rival was Gionna "Liv Morgan" Daddio. Morgan had defeated Rousey during SummerSlam in July 2022, winning the SmackDown Championship. But Rousey didn't give up. In October, she defeated Morgan at the **Extreme** Rules event. Rousey was SmackDown Women's Champion once again.

In 2019, Rousey successfully defended the championship belt against Mercedes "Sasha Banks" Kaestner-Varnado (*top*).

43

CHAPTER 10

A LEGENDARY PIONEER

Rousey started as a judoka, then became a UFC **legend**. To many fans, she is wrestling royalty, and she continues to fight in WWE. As one of the biggest names in three sports, Rousey is an **inspiration** to other fighters and wrestlers like her.

XTREME CHALLENGE

TAKE THE QUIZ BELOW AND PUT WHAT YOU'VE LEARNED TO THE TEST!

1) Why do you think it's important for there to be female wrestlers in WWE?

2) What sport did Rousey win an Olympic medal in?

3) Rousey was inspired by Roderick "'Rowdy' Roddy Piper" Toombs. What athletes inspire you?

4) Who did Rousey lose to in her first WWE match without a partner?

5) Which famous wrestler did Rousey help at WrestleMania XXXI?

GLOSSARY

arena—an enclosed area used for public entertainment.

athlete—someone who plays sports or games that require strength, speed, or agility.

backstage—an area behind the stage of a performance space.

debut—a first appearance.

defend—to retain or seek to retain something, such as a title or position, against a challenge in a contest.

extreme—exceeding the ordinary or expected.

grief—deep sorrow.

induct—to admit as a member.

inspiration—a thing or person that makes someone feel positive.

judo—a sport developed from jujitsu in which opponents attempt to throw each other by using quick movements and leverage.

legacy—the long-lasting impact of a person's life.

legend—a famous or important person, place, or thing that is known for doing something very well.

martial arts—any of several arts of combat and self-defense that are practiced as a sport.

Olympics—a series of international athletic contests held in a different country during the summer and the winter once every four years. Something relating to the Olympics is Olympic.

reverse—to go or cause to go in the opposite direction.

stunt—an unusual or daring action used to gain attention.

ONLINE RESOURCES

To learn more about Ronda Rousey, please visit **abdobooklinks.com** or scan this QR code. These links are routinely monitored and updated to provide the most current information available.

INDEX